Reason Why Advertising

with Intensive Advertising

by John E. Kennedy

Cover photo: Suneel Yadkikar

Table of Contents

Forward..4
Reason Why Advertising..6
  You Must Do the Sum to Prove It - Article I...........................6
  How to Test General Advertising - Article II..........................9
  How to Test Mail-Order Advertising - Article III....................11
  The"Record of Results - Article IV......................................15
  To Whom Are You Advertising? - Article V............................17
  The Responsive Chord in Advertising - Article VI...................20
  Why Some Advertisers Grow Wealthy While Others Fail - Article
    VII...25
  Let There Be Light - Article VIII..30
  Fortunes Wasted in Following "WILL-o'-THE-WISPS" - Article IX 34
  How Shall We Know Good Copy? - Article X.........................38
  They Who Blindly Follow the Blind - Article XI......................40
  Making Sure of Results from General Advertising..................46
Intensive Advertising..50
  Intensive Advertising Defined - Chapter 1...........................50
  Salesmanship Multiplied - Chapter 2.................................52
  Good Advertising is News - Chapter 3................................54
  How Short Should an Ad Be? - Chapter 4............................57
  To Plan and Write Strong Ads - Chapter 5..........................61
Resources...66
  Bonus...67

Talks On Advertising

Space Buying.

RECORD OF RESULTS

HERE is a Cabinet of Data which cost over $100,000 to secure.

This data is in manuscript, and no *duplicate* of it exists.

It embodies an accurate "Record of Results" gained from over 200 kinds of copy, used competitively for 26 different mail order accounts.

A ten-day perusal of this data, with the copy" it indexes to, would be worth a small fortune to certain large Advertisers who now spend avy appropriations for "General Publicity."

But, this Cabinet of Data is an *asset* as valuable almost as the firm name of Lord & Thomas.

Moreover, it stands for just *what* that firm stands for, viz.: *Accumulated Experience* in advertising.

It is to us, and indirectly to our 327 Clients, that the Compass is to the Mariner at Sea.

It is, we believe, the *only* complete summary Advertising *Results* extant, — a Reference Work beyond all price in framing up Advertising Copy, it in choosing the mediums that are thus proven best fit certain classes of Advertised Proposition.

The "Record of Results" has been compiled on Tests made largely in the manner indicated the second and third chapters of our "Book Advertising Tests" recently published.

Without what that "Record of Results" stands , viz.: *Practical Recorded Experience*, all Advertising must be mere guesswork, Opinion, and a series of Gambling to the Advertiser.

No *Individual* Advertiser recording ever so refully the Records from a *single* advertised

proposition, could arrive at a tithe of the *accuracy* this compilation of Records from 26 different Accounts affords.

And no *other* Advertising Agency in America possesses such an *accurate* Index to *Copy Values* and to *selection of mediums*.

The *precise knowledge* this $100,000 Cabinet affords is what *compels* us to pay $72,000 yearly for a staff of Copy-writers who are *capable* of producing "Salesmanship-on-Paper" up to the standard this File of Records *proves* necessary.

This precise knowledge derived from the "Record of Results" is also what enables *us* to choose intelligently between the Publications and Mediums that *claim* your patronage *because other large Advertisers patronize them*, and the Mediums that actually *produce* the *most Results*, for you, per dollar invested.

We do not judge mediums by what their publishers claim in circulation or prestige for them, but by what the recorded *evidence* in our "Record of Results" clearly *proves* they *can perform* for the cost of their space.

And, without such a sure means of selecting the most *profitable* mediums, for each kind of Advertised proposition we could *not dare* propose the Tests on Advertising Service against all competitors, which we voluntarily define in our "Book of Advertising Tests" on pages 17 and 28.

This voluntary definition of a Selling Test, on Results from Advertising, is the strongest proof of Good-faith, and Ability, in the purchasing of Space that any Advertising Agency could offer.

That no *other* Advertising Agency has ever volunteered *such* a test for *Results*, should impress Advertisers as an eloquent fact well worth *quoting*, when the subject of *Space-purchasing* is under discussion.

Without costing *you* a cent, Mr. Advertiser, *you* may share in all the *advantages* this "Record of Results" affords in Space-purchasing, Campaign planning and Copy Writing, provided you "place" your advertising through Lord & Thomas for a trial term.

Say *when* you will discuss this "Record of Results" with us and be shown a sample sheet from its files.

Our $5.00 "Book of Advertising Tests" will be sent free, on request, to any General Advertiser, Mail Order Advertiser, or Wholesale Salesman, who requests it in time.

The Edition is nearly exhausted already—so write for a copy today if you want it.

LORD & THOMAS
Largest Advertising Agency in America

CHICAGO   Established 1873   NEW YORK

Forward

The unknown scene in Advertising and modern marketing is that effective basics only a few use today were actually known since the early 1900's.

It's not too surprising, even though these techniques are now over a hundred years old, that they are still as effective – after all, human nature hasn't changed in our thousands of years of recorded history. What worked then will work now – updated only in language, but not approach.

In the pages following, you will see the origin of "split-tests", "demographics", and "conversions" - along with warnings about following fads. These texts presaged Claude Hopkins' classic "Scientific Advertising." (Hopkins, like Kennedy, also got his fame working at Lord & Thomas.)

John E. Kennedy was one of the earliest known copywriters, who coined the definition of advertising as "Salesmanship In Print." It was he who clued in Albert Lasker to the concept – who used it to generate more income than anyone else in advertising history.

This simple concept revolutionized the industry, which before had been simply offices which ordered ad space in papers – often only listing simply the advertiser's name.

Kennedy then saw that the ideal advertisement wasn't about keeping the public aware of the brand name, but could be required *to get results which could be tracked*. He introduced accountability – which still seems an unknown concept to many in today's marketing offices.

Kennedy saw that the advertisement needed to be written to appeal to the intended reader. It needed to be written so that the reader would consider it worth reading.

This comes to the sole reason for this Masters of Marketing book series. What has been passed off as copywriting and advertising today has mostly forgotten or ignored what Kennedy discovered a century ago. So we bring this series of the classic books back into print and as ebooks so that a hundred years later, we can again educate marketers on how to create effective salesmanship in print – that actually gets sales and can prove it.

The first book Kennedy wrote was a series of articles originally published in "Judicious Advertising." Their common theme being that all advertising should be tested – something Kennedy had brought with him from his days of writing for Dr. Shoop's Restorative.

The articles were later collected and published by Lasker as a small booklet called "The Book of Advertising Tests," which was then sent out to anyone who was interested. The booklet was promoted through free space donated by friendly newspapers and magazines. It wasn't uncommon to have hundreds of inquiries each week from manufacturers, eager to learn this new method of advertising.

The other base concept pushed through Kennedy's first book was that *people need to be given a reason why they should buy.* While this was a new idea to advertising at the time, and often credited to Kennedy it may have come from John E. Powers who also worked at Lord & Thomas.

As Ad Age explains: "While early admen Charles Bates and John E. Powers were committed to reason-why advertising, Canadian-born Kennedy exploited this approach to its fullest. In 1904, Kennedy's definition of advertising: "Salesmanship in print," impressed Albert Lasker, as did Kennedy's graphically distinctive ads with no-nonsense, hard-hitting copy. Named L&T's chief copywriter, Kennedy set out to learn everything about his clients' businesses, develop selling points and test copy. Lasker published his ideas in "The Booklet of Advertising Tests," sent copies to business prospects and based L&T's creative work on his philosophy."

In 1914, Kennedy was paid $25,000 by a group of publishers to write a report ("Intensive Advertising") on what could be done to improve advertising.

You will see in this, among other basic concepts, the beginning of *campaigns*, where the company and even a line of goods would be "branded" by a consistent look and feel of the ads.

But let me get out of your way so you can enjoy the genius of Kennedy, just as it was when he wrote it – as we take you back to 1904 as a young copywriter tells the world how to write their ads, what to put in them, and why...

Dr. Robert C. Worstell

March 2014

Reason Why Advertising

A Group of Articles that Actually Say Something About Advertising

BY LORD & THOMAS

CHICAGO AND NEW YORK

Originally published in 1905 as "The Book of Advertising Tests"

You Must Do the Sum to Prove It - Article I

ADVERTISING should be judged only by the goods it is conclusively known to sell, at a given cost.

Mere opinions on Advertising Copy should be excluded from consideration, because opinions on Advertising are conflicting as opinions on Religion.

Forty per cent of all the people in the world are Buddhists, and are of opinion that Buddhism is the only true religion. Twelve per cent of the world's people being Roman Catholics, are firm in the opinion that the remaining 88 per cent are wrong, and sure of damnation accordingly.

Eight per cent of the world's people being Protestants believe that both the Buddhists and Catholics, and all others, are deplorably ignorant of the only true faith, which of course must be their own particular sect of Protestantism.

And, neither Buddhist, Catholic, nor Protestant, can convince the 2 per cent of Jews that their opinion is wrong and should be changed.

That is a side-light on the inconsistency of mere Opinion.

Religion must continue in the realm of opinion, because no one can decide which Creed is right, and which wrong, till he dies and finds out the facts for himself.

And, no mere man who died has ever come back to Earth to settle the dispute.

***

But, it is different with Advertising, as it is with Mechanics or with Medicine, all three of which can be conclusively tested.

Many Advertisers, however, seem satisfied to spend their money on mere Opinions about Advertising when they might have invested it on Evidence about Advertising.

These are the Advertisers whose business must die before they can be convinced that "General Publicity" (merely "Keeping-the-Name-before-the-People") is wrong and "Salesmanship-on-paper" right.

They blindly gamble in Advertising when they might have safely invested in it.

If they were to buy any other kind of Service, except Advertising, they would demand tangible proof of its efficacy before they spent much money on it.

If they hired a Salesman, for instance, they would expect him to prove he was earning his salary by making a satisfactory "Record on Sales."

They would not accept, for long, statements from him that he was "Making a General Impression on the Trade" for his salary.

Nor would they be satisfied with the statement that he was "Keeping-the-Name before-the-People" profitably enough to compensate for lack of Sales.

Nor would they enthuse over a report from him that he was "Influencing Sales" for their other salesmen.

What the Advertising Employer would demand from his Salesman would be profitable Orders. He would demand Sales, clearly made by the Salesman himself, each sale carrying a given profit over cost for the Employer.

That is just what the Advertising Employer should demand from his Advertising Expenditure too — Sales — proven Sales, carrying a satisfactory profit.

And, if he insists upon it he can get the kind of Advertising which will actually produce Sales instead of a vague "General Influence on Sales." Because, true Advertising is only "Salesmanship-on-paper" after all.

When it is anything less than Salesmanship it is not real Advertising, but only "General Publicity."

And, "General Publicity" admittedly claims only to "Keep the Name before the People," — to produce a "General impression on the Trade," and to "Influence Sales" for the salesmen.

It makes the same lame excuses as would be made by a Salesman who failed to earn his salary in actually selling goods.

***

But, "General Publicity," or any other Advertising, should be judged by the self-same standards as the Salesman is judged, viz., by the goods it is clearly proven to sell at a given cost per dollar invested in it.

We are stating this matter very definitely, so you will see that we, at least, make no attempt to evade the Main Issue.

If the Advertising Service we sell you does not positively Sell goods, and do it profitably, we admit that it is doing nothing else for you which is worth its cost.

And, We are the only Advertising Concern in America who are willing to be judged by this definition of Advertising.

Because, We are the only Advertising Concern in America which pays the necessary price for Skill and Experience to produce able 'Salesmanship-on-paper" in place of vague " General Publicity."

Moreover, We are the only Advertising Concern in America, or elsewhere, who volunteer a "Test" by which the Results from our own, as well as from other Advertising, may be accurately gauged.

We have an established business of Several Million Dollars per annum at stake in this Test — the largest Advertising business in the world to-day.

Could we afford to supply you, Mr. Advertiser, with a means of disproving our claims for Lord & Thomas's "Salesmanship-on-paper " if these claims were based on anything less than the bed-rock of actual Certainty?

We repeat that the only way to judge Advertising is to judge it by the amount of goods It is conclusively known to Sell, at a given cost.

And, in the following article we supply you a means of positively testing Lord & Thomas's "Salesmanship-on-paper," in competition with any other kind of Advertising.

Could we prove our faith in any more tangible form than this?

How to Test General Advertising - Article II

SELECT two Cities of about the same population, in approximately the same climate, and with equally good newspapers.

St. Paul and Minneapolis are fair examples , — but scores of other equivalents can be named or chosen.

Check up carefully the quantity of your Advertised Goods in these two cities which the Retailers have on hand at a given date. Then ask them to keep"Record (on a blank form you supply) of the goods in your advertised lines which they will stock within the next four months.

Then, run in one of the two competitive cities the Advertising Copy you have already been using, as supplied by your present Advertising Agency.

At the same time run in the other competitive city Lord & Thomas's "Salesmanship-on-paper" copy.

Spend for each kind exactly the same appropriation, and make it sufficiently liberal to show some results on the second month.

Continue this competitive copy for four months, which is the minimum time on which General Advertising can be made to produce a fair measure of Results.

Then, on a certain day, send out enough men to check up the amount of your Advertised goods in the hands of each Retailer at the end of the four months.

Add to the goods on hand at time of starting test the goods since stocked in each City. Then subtract from this total the Advertised goods remaining on the Retailers' hands in each City at end of the four, months Advertising test.

The difference between will show the quantity of your Advertised goods actually sold to Consumers, in each city, during the four months period of actual selling test.

The difference between the Value of goods sold in each City during the test period will then be a reliable index to the relative Selling Power of the two Competing kinds of Advertising used.

Now, cross the copy in each City for four months longer.

Use Lord & Thomas's "Salesmanship-on-paper" in the City where you previously used your current Advertising Copy, and vice versa.

Check up the goods on hand at end of the second four months again, as before.

When you find the difference in Sales (with the same expenditure for Advertising) to be heavily in favor of Lord & Thomas's copy (as in the first four months), you will have made a Copy Test, that may save you over 40 per cent of your National appropriation every year afterwards.

This test may seem a lot of trouble to undertake at first sight.

But, is not 40 per cent per annum, of your Advertising Appropriation, worth that trouble?

And, what is it worth to know conclusively for all time, the relative value of "General Publicity" as actually compared with Lord & Thomas's Salesmanship-on-paper in a downright Selling Test ?

We have proven a difference of 66 per cent between two such kinds of Copy on equivalent tests.

Isn't that a difference to make you sit up and think hard about Copy?

When will you talk with us about Salesmanship-on-paper ?

How to Test Mail-Order Advertising - Article III

CHOOSE a list of Standard Magazines, for a representative month's Advertising.

Run your Current copy in half the number of these magazines for that month.

Key each advertisement, in each magazine, separately so you will know just which advertisement and which magazine each Inquiry results from.

Then, run Lord & Thomas's "Salesmanship-on-paper" copy in the remaining half of the magazines, keying each advertisement separately, in each magazine, so you will know which advertisement as and which medium each Inquiry comes from.

By "keying" is meant that you change the reply address in each advertisement, and in each magazine.

Thus, in Munsey's you say "Address 86 State St." ; in Everybody's, "75 State St."; and in McCall's Magazine you say "6th floor 86 State St." ; while in another you say "8th floor 75 State St.," for instance.

By arrangement with the Post Office all replies to these different addresses will be put into your Letter-box, regardless of street address on envelope.

Now, you can tell by the envelope address on each Reply or Inquiry which magazine, and which particular advertisement in that magazine, produced it.

Then, when the Inquiries from the competing advertisements cease coming, you can total up the number of Inquiries each magazine produced from each particular advertisement.

Now, having the total number of Inquiries from each individual advertisement, you divide that number into the cost of the Space used for each piece of copy, in each magazine.

This will give you the exact cost, per Inquiry, from each separate piece of copy, in each magazine.

The cost per Inquiry with your own current Copy, may then be intelligently compared with the cost per Inquiry through Lord & Thomas's "Salesman-ship-on-paper."

***

Now, cross the copy for the second Month's Advertising Test.

By this is meant, — insert your own current Copy which appeared last month in Munsey 's, in this month's Everybody's, for instance.

And, the Lord & Thomas copy which appeared last month in Everybody's you now insert in Munsey's of this month.

This gives a fair distribution of Mediums to each competing Advertisement.

When the Inquiries cease coming from this second month's insertion, make the same"Record as before of Cost per Inquiry, for each piece of competing copy from each magazine.

Then, add the total number of Inquiries obtained from your own current Copy, during both months, together.

Then divide that total number into the total expenditure for Space used in publication of that Copy.

This will give the average cost per Inquiry, with the kind of Copy you have been regularly using.

Now, compare this with the average cost per Inquiry obtained from the same magazines, at the same identical periods, with Lord & Thomas's "Salesmanship-on-paper."

The difference between the cost per Inquiry with the two kinds of Copy will then be a reliable Index to the relative Earning Power of the two competing kinds of copy.

Now, use the same "Follow-up" (Booklets and Letters) , on all the Inquiries from both Sources.

The percentage of Sales which results from each of the two competitive groups of Inquiries and Follow-up will then determine the relative Profits to the Advertiser from each kind of Copy.

***

No Test on earth can be more conclusive than this, and none is easier made.

And, what such a Test will reveal (in difference between Results from two different kinds of Copy) will "stagger"you, as it once did us.

An extensive series of such Tests, carried over a long period of Time, with many differing propositions, has proved up to us a fine consistency in Results.

We have found, from such continuous Tests registered in our *'"Record of Results,"

that the kind of Advertising which sells Washing Machines by mail at one-third the cost other Copy sells them, will, when applied according to the individual needs of the different articles, also sell Ear Drums by mail, Violins, Shoes, or Pianos, in about the same ratio.

Moreover, we have found that the "something" in Copy which sells these Goods by Mail, at one-half to one-third the cost other Copy sells them, will also sell them through Retailers, over the Counter.

That "something" is Selling-Force, -- Conviction saturated into the Copy, with sound Reasons-Why.

It is the salient *' something" which makes some Advertisers millionaires in a few years, while other Advertisers, spending the same amount of money for equally good propositions, "go broke."

The kind of Advertising which will work these Miracles of Success may be the very kind you like least, and quite contrary to your present preference.

But, Advertising is not originally intended to merely please your fancy, Mr. Advertiser.

Its first, last, and only duty is to Sell Goods, and to sell them cheaper than they can be sold without it, and cheaper than they can be sold by any other kind of Advertising.

That kind of Advertising, which will do this, viz., ** Salesmanship-on-paper," is the only kind we want to supply you.

It is based not on what we like best to read, but on what our "Record of Results" proves will sell the most Goods to Readers, per dollar of outlay.

We make no attempt to merely please you, Mr. Advertiser, with Copy. We can't afford to cater to any whim or hobby (if you have any) which our"Records indicate would clearly waste Space that should be used in selling goods instead.

Because, we agree that the Service we supply shall be judged by the Results it produces and by no other Standard.

That being the case, we cannot afford to use any but the kind of Copy our "Records of Results" has proven to be the only Advertising sure to produce the right Result every time.

If you won't let us use that kind of Advertising for you we cannot assume responsibility for Results. Because, we can't afford to assume the risk of failure with a kind of Copy which might please you immensely yet prove a total failure in Selling your goods.

You may never know how much you are losing on copy, in cold Dollars and Cents, until you prove up Lord & Thomas' "Salesmanship-on-paper" in competition with the Advertising you are now using.

And, we offer you a chance to prove it up, which may be worth half your annual appropriation, in increased Results from the same expenditure.

Is that sum worth saving?

Then, let us talk the Saving process over together, in a personal interview.

Our "Record of Results" is described in next article.

The"Record of Results - Article IV

HERE is a Cabinet of Data which cost over $100,000 to Secure. (Opposite page.) This data is in manuscript, and no duplicate of it exists. It embodies an accurate "Record of Results" obtained from hundreds of kinds of copy, used competitively for different Mail-Order accounts.

A ten-day perusal of this data, with the "Copy" it indexes to, would be worth a small fortune to certain large Advertisers who now spend heavy appropriations for "General Publicity."

But, this cabinet of data is an Asset, as valuable almost as the firm name of Lord & Thomas.

Moreover, it stands for just what that firm name stands for; viz., Accumulated Experience in Advertising.

It is to us, and indirectly to our Clients, what the Compass is to the Mariner at Sea.

It is, we believe the only complete summary of Advertising Results extant, — a Reference Work beyond all price in framing up Advertising Copy, and in choosing Mediums that best fit certain classes of advertised propositions.

This "Record of Results" has been compiled from Tests made largely in the manner indicated in the last two chapters.

Without what it stands for, viz. : Practical"Recorded Experience, all Advertising must be mere guess-work. Opinion, and gambling to the Advertiser.

No Individual Advertiser"Recording ever so carefully the"Records from a single advertised proposition, could arrive at a tithe of the accuracy this compilation of"Records from 86 different Accounts affords.

And no other Advertising Concern in America possesses such an accurate Index to Copy Values, and to selection of Mediums.

The precise knowledge this $100,000 Cabinet affords is what compels us to pay $72,000 yearly for a staff of Copy-writers who are capable of producing "Salesmanship-on-paper" up to the standard this File of"Records proves necessary.

No other Advertising Agency in America pays a third of that sum for "Copy-Staff," because no other has the means of knowing absolutely the tremendous difference in Results due to Copy such as ours of to-day.

Without costing you a cent, Mr. Advertiser, you may share in all the advantages this "Record of Results" affords, provided you place your Advertising through Lord & Thomas for a triad term.

Say when you will discuss this "Record of Results"with us, and be shown a sample sheet from its files.

To Whom Are You Advertising? - Article V

MR. ADVERTISER!

You spend your money to tell People what you've got to Sell.

Now, what kind of People can afford to buy your particular Goods?

What income must they possess to be probable Consumers of your Advertised Product?

How many possibilities of Sale has your product per thousand average Readers?

These are all vital factors in the framing up of your campaign, and in the prospects of Success from it.

Here are some Census figures upon which we base our Campaigns and Calculations.

In the year 1900 there were 15,964,000 Families in the United States.

These Families averaged about five persons each, or a total population of 75,994,575.

Fifty-one per cent of that population lived in the Country — 10 2/3 per cent was Semi-urban, and 38 1/3 per cent lived in Cities and Towns.

The Newspapers and Periodicals these Families read had a total circulation of 8,168,148,749 copies per year.

That means 512 copies per year per Family, or nearly two copies per day for each family.

A great deal of Reading, isn't it?

Now comes the astonishing part of the Census figures.

Nearly 33 per cent of all these Families had an average Income of less than $400 per year, or about $80 per capita.

Only 21 per cent of these Families had an annual Income of $400 to $600.

Only 15 per cent of these Families had an annual Income of $600 to $900.

Only 10 1/2 per cent of them had an annual Income of $900 to $1,200.

Only 7 1/2% per cent of them had an annual Income of $1,800 to $3,000.

And, of the Automobile Class, only 5 per cent had an Income of over $3,000 per Family, or $600 per capita.

Now, wouldn't that set you thinking?

Suppose you have Pianos to sell through Advertising, how many Families of the total that read Newspapers and Magazines could afford to buy one?

Then, how many of these are already supplied?

That estimate shows your Possible Market through Advertising, and indicates the way that Market must be approached.

It also shows about how many Readers you must pay to reach who cannot buy your Piano, no matter how much your advertising makes them want it.

And it also shows the futility of writing "Catchy" Copy to attract the greatest number of Readers for your advertisement. What you need is not Numbers of Readers, but Class of Readers. And that very limited class you must convince, when you once get their attention, or you lose all profit from your Piano advertising.

You must make up in Conviction and Selling-force for what you lose in possible number of purchasers with such a proposition.

But, when your product is something which can be used by the Masses, it is then a better subject for Advertising.

Because you then have about 85 per cent more possibilities of Sale, among Average Readers, than you would have had with a Piano or Automobile.

The current mistake in Advertising to this great 85 per cent of Average Families is that of talking over their heads, in terms and thought-forms which are unfamiliar or unintelligible to them.

Observe that not one of this great 85 per cent of families has an Income of more than $1,800 per year, or $360 per person.

Observe also that the Average Income of this great 85 per cent is less than $500 per year, per family, or $100 per head.

We must not expect the Average of such people to have classical educations, nor an excessive appreciation of Art and Inference.

Neither are they as Children in Intellect, nor thick-headed Fools.

They are just Average Americans of good average intelligence, considerable shrewdness, and large bumps of Incredulity . Most of them might have come "from Missouri" because they all have "show me!" ever ready in their minds, when any plausible Advertising Claim is made to them.

But, they are willing to be "Shown" when the arguments are sensible enough, as well as simple enough, to appeal readily to their mental make-up. They are not suffocating for want of pretty pictures and pleasing phrases in Advertising.

What they are most interested in is, "Show me how to get more for my money of what I need for Existence and Comfort rather than for Luxury."

This " great 85 per cent"of Readers has a peculiar Habit-of-Thought or Mental Caliber of its own which responds most freely to a certain well-defined form of approach and reasoning.

We have made as close a study of that average Habit-of-Thought and its proper approach as we have made of the Census data suggested herein.

Our "Record of Results" from Advertising, which has been based on a clear conception of that Mental Caliber, shows that our estimate of it rang true in over 90 per cent of the Copy we have planned and written to reach that average "Habit-of-Thought" most responsively.

We would like to show you some of these Results, contrasted with other Copy written without such guiding data.

The Responsive Chord in Advertising - Article VI

ADVERTISING is just Salesmanship-on-paper.

It is a means of multiplying the work of the Salesman, who writes it, several thousand-fold.

With the salary paid a single Salesman, it is possible, through Advertising, to reach a thousand customers for every one he could have reached orally.

It is also a means of discovering, and developing, new customers where they were not previously known to exist.

These facts are mentioned here because few Business Men have a correct idea of what true Advertising should consist of.

To start with the wrong point-of-view, on an advertising campaign, is to grope and experiment, and to speculate, with an appropriation which should have been invested as intelligently as in merchandise.

True Advertising is just Salesmanship multiplied.

When we multiply nothing by ten thousand we still have nothing as a result.

When we multiply a pretty picture, or a catch-phrase, or the mere name of a firm, or article, a thousand times we still have nothing as a result.

But when we multiply a good, strong, clearly expressed reason-why, a person should buy the article we want to sell, a thousand times, we then have impressed, through advertising, one thousand more people with that reason than if it had been told verbally to one person by the same salesman.

Of course, cold type usually lacks the personal influence of the Salesman and, for this reason, Salesmanship-on-paper needs to be stronger — more convincing and conclusive than it need be by word of mouth.

Besides, when we multiply anything a thousand fold, at a large expense for the mechanical process of doing so, it is wisdom to see that the thing to be multiplied is as nearly perfect as we can get it.

Nothing multiplied by one thousand, costs just the same for the mechanical expense of multiplying it, but the net result is nothing — less that expense.

This is why so many Advertising Campaigns fail.

Because, the Good Folks who spend their money for Space have no definite idea of what should occupy it.

When we clearly understand that Salesmanship alone should fill it, we all know, in a general way, what that means though each of us might go about it in a different way.

Salesmanship-on-paper means convincing Readers that they should buy the article we want to sell.

Many good Salesmen find it impossible to do this convincing on Paper because the customer does not stand before them, with his facial expression as an index to the line of talk the Salesman should use in that particular case.

This is where the creative power of the Salesman-on-paper becomes vitally necessary.

He must, first of all, analyze the proposition thoroughly — master the full details of the thing to be sold, then lay out a strong logical line of argument upon it, "lime-lighting" the good points, and subtly masking the bad ones out of the reader's mental vision.

All this, however, is just what any good Salesman-on-the-Road, or Salesman-in-the-Warehouse, could, should, and probably does, do.

But, a glance at the Advertising pages of current publications will show how mighty few Advertisers adopt even these first principles of Salesmanship in their copy.

However, it is after this that the true genius and power of able Salesmanship-on-paper must be exerted.

That consists in the staging of the arguments, to fit the audience.

A given argument, presented in a certain form of thought and expression, will strike responsively in the minds of a given number, among the class of people aimed at, in each thousand.

If that per cent be high, it means large profit to the Advertiser — large returns.

If that per cent be low, it means that the advertisement has not convinced, has not struck responsively upon the particular class for whom the article advertised is best adapted, notwithstanding the sound argument used.

This peculiarly "Responsive " quality in an Advertisement may be called its Personality.

Observe that it may not be the Personality of the Writer at all, but the Personality which he estimates will best fit the particular class of people who compose the largest field of sale for the article advertised.

This intangible Personality feature may be likened to the keynote of a church, or of a music hall.

It is well known that every such building will respond most fully (in sound) to some one particular musical note of the scale, in proportion to the interior size and shape of the structure.

Thus, a note which sounds full, clear, and vibrant in one such edifice, will sound thin, flat, and harsh in another.

Because, it is not the Responsive Chord of the second building, as it is of the first.

The Musician who could look at the inside of a church, then declare its Responsive Chord, from an estimate, would be in kindred position to the Advertising Writer who could most profitably fit the Personality of his Salesmanship-on-paper to the class he aims at.

To strike the Responsive Chord full and true, with that class, would mean 100 per cent in possible results, from the arguments deduced.

To strike a chord which sounded harsh, uncongenial, or unfamiliar, to that class would be to arouse latent antagonism or distrust.

Either of these would discount the effect of the same logic, from 25 to 90 per cent.

This is why the successful Salesman-on-paper must possess Imagination, as well as logic.

He must be able to form a clear conception of the class he aims to convince.

He must estimate how the average mind of that class is likely to work, under a certain argument, and under a certain mode of expressing it.

Then, he must be able to create the Personality, in his mode of expression, which will Strike the most Responsive Chord with the greatest possible number.

Some few Advertisers possess this power of creating a personality which fits responsively the mass of humanity — the great 85 per cent.

That "David Harum" type of Personality is well exemplified in the copy personally written by Mr. C. W. Post, the Grape-Nuts and Postum Manufacturer of Battle Creek.

That his colossal business (netting over a million dollars yearly in profits on these two advertised Cereals) , is chiefly due to that "Responsive Chord"in his advertising, is a vivid fact.

This ability to estimate the average mentality, and Habit-of -Thought, of the Class aimed at, with the power to create a Personality in the copy which will fit it most agreeably and familiarly, is what the Salesman-on-paper must have, in addition to the logical arguments of the Salesman in any other field.

The difference in Results between copy written by two equally bright men may be, and often is, 80 per cent, though the same space be used in each case, to sell the self-same article.

That difference consists, first of all, in the quality of argument, the "Reason-why"

that each of the two lines of copy contains, and next in the Personality with which these arguments have been invested, in either copy, so as to strike the most Responsive Chord with the class of readers aimed at.

It is doubtful if this faculty of taking the Mental Measure of a given class, and gauging their Habit-of-Thought, can be acquired where it does not naturally exist.

Because, it is a sort of Instinct, such as guides the Timber-Explorer, who will travel a hundred square miles of forest, and estimate closely just how many thousand feet of timber are on it, though he never counts a tree.

That sales of timber lands running into over millions of dollars, have been regularly made on this instinctive knowledge of a single man, is evidence of the general accuracy, and reliability, of such trained, and instinctive estimates.

This same Faculty has more to do with successful Salesmanship-on-paper than is generally recognized. And it is rare enough to be interesting.

We found it so when we had to purchase enough of it to serve our clients.

And, we pay a salary of $72,000 per year to a Copy-Staff which can use this faculty in conjunction with our "Record of Results."

That is three times the Salary paid to a Copy-Staff by any other Advertising Agency in America.

And that $72,000 Copy-Staff, with the"Recorded experience of 20 years to guide it, is at the service of every Lord & Thomas client. Let us tell you more about this verbally.

LORD & THOMAS.

Why Some Advertisers Grow Wealthy While Others Fail - Article VII

SIXTY PER CENT of all Advertisers fail!

Because, they spend their money for Space, under the delusion that Space filled with anything "Catchy" is "Advertising."

They believe "Money Talks" in Advertising, even when it says nothing.

They forget that Space costs the same whether we fill it with Pictured Nothings or with enduring Convictions.

And, the difference, in Results, between two kinds of **copy," costing the same for space, in a single advertisement, has often exceeded 80 per cent, as our"Records on tests prove.

General Advertisers, who have no means of tracing direct results, and who spend their money for "General Publicity," will smile at this.

But, Mail-Order Advertisers know it is true.

The "1900 Washer Co.," of Binghamton, N. Y., or the Wilson Ear Drum Co., of Louisville, for instance, could afford to smile at Advertisers who doubt its being true.

These are the kind of Advertisers to whom Advertising is not a blind speculation, but systematic eye-open investment.

Their"Records show the precise cost of every inquiry for their goods through advertising, because their every Advertisement in every Medium is separately keyed.

They can thus gauge accurately the relative earning power of each separate bit of copy published at their expense, and of each medium in which that copy has been inserted.

They thus know what kind to avoid, as well as what kind to use.

Please note that the Lord & Thomas definition of "General Publicity" is "Keeping-the-Name-before-the-People."

When we speak of "General Advertising" we mean copy which sells goods through the Retailer. This latter class of advertising constitutes three-fourths of our business.

And note also that we are NOT "advising" General Advertisers to GO INTO MAIL-ORDER BUSINESS.

WE DO, however, strongly insist that all Copy for GENERAL ADVERTISING should possess as much positive SELLING-FORCE and CONVICTION as it would NEED to actually and profitably SELL Goods direct BY MAIL.

Here is the actual experience of a well-known national Advertiser, who sells a $5.00 article by mail only.

This Advertiser has proved that a certain fixed average per cent of his Inquiries convert into direct sales through his "follow-up" system.

Each Inquiry is therefore worth a certain fixed price to him which he can pay with profit.

One single piece of copy has been run for that Advertiser, practically without change, in all mediums used, for over two years. About $200,000 has been spent in repeated publication of that single bit of copy. Why?

Because, it produced results (Inquiries) at lower cost than any other copy ever run for them in eight years, until lately.

The first month Inquiries from it cost (say) 85 cents each.

Repetition, for two years, wore out some of its interest, so that Inquiries from it finally cost an average of (say) $1.00 each. New "copy" had been tried a great many times, written by many different ad-smiths, but no other ad ever produced the Inquiries at less than $2.85 average, till lately.

Some of the copy that looked good enough to try, cost $14.20 per Inquiry. And that was better looking copy than half of what fills "General Publicity" space in costly mediums at this very minute.

Consider what the knowledge derived from a large collection of certified data, like the above, means when placed at the disposal of General Advertisers who now "go it blind" on copy.

If the $5.00 article had been sold through Retailers, in the usual way, without accurate means of checking results from every advertisement, it is more than probable that the $14.20 kind of copy would have been used continuously.

Because, that was the catchy" kind, so much in favor at this very minute with "General Publicity" Advertisers.

And, it would have been considered good copy so long as the salesmen did its work in addition to their own, the General Results being credited in a general way to "General Publicity."

But, it would clearly have required fourteen times as much of that "$14.20 kind"of alleged "Advertising" to produce the same amount of selling effect upon the public as the "85 cent kind" of copy (which averaged about $1.00 per inquiry over the two years) actually did produce.

Let us figure this out more conclusively : The Blank Company spent $75,000 per year, for space, with copy producing Inquiries at about $1.00 average.

It would thus have cost them about fourteen times as much, or $1,050,000 per year, to sell as many of their $5.00 articles through the $14.20 kind of "catchy" copy as it actually did cost them to sell the same quantity with the $1.00 average kind of copy.

Good Reader, get that thought clearly into your mind, for we're talking cold facts now, — facts we can verify to any prospective client.

What was it worth to the Blank Company to get a new advertisement which would pull Inquiries at the old rate of 85 cents each, when their most successful copy had worn out, after two years' use, so that Inquiries were finally costing them $1.25 average?

Figure it out and you'll see that one single piece of such copy would be worth a third of their $75,000 yearly appropriation, viz., $25,000.

Because, it would add a third to what their appropriation is solely spent for, viz. , Inquiries for their goods.

But Lord & Thomas "Reason-why" Copy did better than that, when applied.

It reduced the cost of Inquiries, for the selfsame $5.00 article, to 41 cents average, during all the months it has been running. Now Reflect what similar treatment with your appropriation would mean to you, Mr. Advertiser !

The earning power of every dollar trebled by the mere substitution of Lord & Thomas 's "Salesmanship-on-paper"for the best copy the Advertiser had in ten years prior to that substitution.

An Advertising appropriation of $75,000 made equal in proven earning power to what $225,000 would have earned, with the copy which preceded it, and which was producing Inquiries at $1.25.

That single piece of Lord & Thomas copy, which ran practically without change for about four months, had in that time produced approximately 60,976 Inquiries.

These are worth $1.25 each to the Advertiser, or $91,464 in all, though we reduced their cost to 41 cents each with an actual outlay of about $25,000.

In four months that one piece of copy has thus earned $66,466 more for the Advertiser than the $1.25 kind of Copy used immediately before it had produced from the same investment.

And, what made it pull Inquiries by mail is precisely what would make it produce Inquiries verbally for the goods, through Retailers, by the use of Lord & Thomas's "Reason-why" and Conviction in the Copy.

This, Mr. Advertiser, is only one of many actual instances that we can prove up to Advertisers who agree to place their appropriations through us, provided we do thus prove up our capacity to increase Results, with their present appropriations.

Other Advertising Agents will belittle this statement because they do not know what we do about comparative Results from actual Tests on Copy, such as we have made.

They cannot know what our "Salesmanship-on-paper" is capable of doing.

Because they have never had the equipment to produce it, nor the organization to"Record and compare Results from it with "General Publicity" results, in such a way as to provide a reliable guide for the writing of future Copy.

Moreover, it is not their money that pays for the space they fill with "General Publicity,"— the "$14.20" kind of Copy.

They risk nothing in any case. Their commission is just as safe when they fill your space with cheap and catchy "General Publicity" as it would be if they filled it with that reliable "Salesmanship-on-paper," which produces results for " 41 cents"as against $14.20.

But, — how can you hope to compete if using such ** $14.20 "copy against your competitor who may pit our "41 cent"kind of copy against you?

Not one Advertising Agency in America pays a third what we do (viz., $72,000 per year in Salaries) for a capable Copy-Staff.

Not three, in America, pay individually a fifth of what we pay for Copy.

Three-fourths of what other Agencies spend for "Service" is paid to able Solicitors who simply sell you Space but cannot help you to fill that space with the kind of Copy that brings you back large profit on the outlay.

Not a fifth of what other Agencies pay for "Service" is invested in the Copy, which alone determines how profitable or unprofitable that space be made for you.

The Advertising world is waking up to this fact, Mr. Advertiser, and don't forget that It IS we — Lord & Thomas — who are doing the awakening.

Could we afford to raise this disturbing question, on the tremendous importance of "Copy," if we were not the best equipped Advertising Concern in America to produce the kind we are talking about, for Clients who want it?

We have cited a Mail-Order proposition in this article simply because it provided a simple example of traceable results, on one kind of Test.

But, we have proved that what makes Copy sell goods by Mail makes it sell them, in equal ratio, through Retailers, over the counter by General Advertising.

Our article herein on "Making Sure of Results from General Advertising"explains this phase of the subject clearly.

Let There Be Light - Article VIII

NOW, Mr. Advertiser, let us be frank!

Let us look at this subject of Advertising squarely, and dissect it.

Let us discard all prejudice or predilection, and accept only Evidence, in our final investigation.

Let us cut out sentiment, precedent, and "Popular Opinion," and treat the subject as though we had never heard of it before and "came from Missouri." If, for instance, we had a load of Hay to sell how would we attempt to sell it?

Would we show our customers the Daisies that grew in it, ask them to note the style of the loading, the fine pair of horses that draw it, and the Vandyke beard of the Driver?

Would we tell him this is the same kind of Hay as was raked by "Maud Muller on a Summer's day" in Whittier's poem?

Guess not! — eh?

We'd tell him of the nutritious qualities that particular load of Hay possessed, for the feeding of horses, and then we'd name the price, delivered, show why the hay was worth it, and let it go at that.

***

Now, if our customer lived at a distance, and we must sell him the Hay by letter, how would we proceed?

Quote "Maud Muller" to him — then refer to the Daisies, the Horses, and Beard?

No, sir — not for a moment!

We would confine ourselves carefully to the feeding qualities of our Hay, and to the advantages of buying while the price was right.

Now, suppose we had five hundred loads of this Hay to sell, instead of one load, and did, not know just where to write to in order to sell it.

That's when we'd Advertise!

But does the fact of our going into Print mean that we must go into Literature, Art, or Clever Conceits in space-filling too, in order to sell our Hay through Advertising?

Are we not still trying to sell just Horse-feed? How can we expect the picture of "Maud Muller on a Summer's Day" to help us close a deal with an unpoetical party who has Horses to Feed, and must do it economically?

The Horse owner knows good Hay when he sees it, and he will know it from description almost as well as from sight.

When he needs good Hay then the most interesting thing we can tell him is a description of the Hay we have to sell, and why it is good, and why it is worth the price.

No amount of Maud Muller picture, or "Association of Ideas" will sell him Hay so surely and quickly as plain Hay-talk and Horse-sense.

***

But you will be told, Mr. Advertiser, that "in order for an Advertisement to sell goods it must first be seen and read!" You will also be told that "in the mass of reading matter surrounding your Advertisement your Space must be made more 'attractive' than the rest, in order to be seen and read by the largest possible number."

Now, at first sight this line of talk looks logical enough, but how does it dissect?

Suppose you have a pretty Maud Muller advertisement about your Hay, with a fancy border of Daisies all around it, and a delicate vignette of "the Judge looking back as he climbed the hill!" You would certainly attract the attention of many more Readers with that ad than with a bald caption of "Hay delivered, at $8.00 a ton."

But the man who wants Hay is the only party you can get back the cost of your advertising from, and you can interest him more intensely with the Hay caption than with all the "Maud Muller" kind of ads in the magazines.

And, you can afford to lose the "attention" of 400,000 Readers who have no use for Hay, if you can clinch sales for your five hundred loads with the few people who do need it.

Observe that it is not necessary to "attract the attention" of every Reader in a 430,000 circulation, in order to sell 500 loads of Hay.

But it is vitally necessary that you convince, at least, five hundred probable Purchasers that you have the kind of Hay they need, at the price they can afford to pay for it.

If an advertisement, in a circulation of 430,000, costs $60 and we have a profit of $1.00 per load on Hay, we need only sell one load each to sixty people in order to pay expenses.

But, if we "attract the attention" of 80,000 people by our advertisement, and sell only thirty loads of Hay to them, we would then be out $30, and must credit the balance of our Advertising investment to "General Publicity "—to "Keeping-the Name-before-the-People " -- etc. , in the vague hope that some other day these people may perhaps buy Hay from us, if we then have it to sell.

That mistaken idea of "Attracting the Attention of the greatest number, for a given price" is what costs fortunes to Advertisers annually.

The striving to "Attract Attention" instead of striving to positively Sell Goods is the basis of all Advertising misunderstanding.

So long as "Attracting Attention" remains the aim of Advertisers, so long will the process of attracting it remain in the hands of Advertising Men who affect the Literary and Artistic attitude, rather than the plain logical convincing attitude of the "Salesman-on-paper." And, great are the Advertising Writers' temptations to use "Attractive" copy at the expense of Convincing copy.

Because, great is the temptation to be considered "smart," bright," "catchy," "Literary, " "artistic," " dignified," "High-grade," etc.

There is popular applause for the Writer of catchy "General Publicity," which "attracts attention" even though it does not sell goods.

But, there is no applause for the Writer of prosaic "Salesmanship - on - paper," which is forceful enough, and convincing enough to sell goods, but so simple to understand as to seem easy.

This is one reason-why "Catchy" Advertising is so current, and true "Salesmanship-on-paper " so rare.

Another reason is the far greater cost to produce studied "Salesmanship-on-paper" than to produce four times as much catchy "General Publicity."

A still further reason is that the Makers of "General Publicity" know they can never be held to account for definite results from that kind of Copy, because nothing definite is promised through it.

— To "Keep-the-Name-before-the-People." — To "Make a General Impression on the Trade, and on the Public." — To "Influence Sales." — To "Protect the Market."

These are the vague nothings promised you by the Makers of "General Publicity," Mr. Advertiser.

These are the fractional parts of Advertising you get in return for an outlay which could have brought you back 150 per cent instead of 30 per cent of the outlay for Space.

Remember, Mr. Advertiser, that Lord & Thomas's "Salesmanship-on-paper" will do all that '^General Publicity" can do toward "Keeping - the - Name - before - the - People," "Creating a General Impression on the Trade," etc.

And, in addition to this, it will actually, positively, and conclusively Sell Goods through Retailers, or by Mail, in sufficient volume to pay 50 to 300 per cent on the investment in Space it occupies.

Nearly every Advertising Agency to whom you might show this article would promise all that it outlines, and fulfill that promise with the kind of "copy" they are now supplying other advertisers.

But don't forget that in order to "deliver the goods" it is first necessary to have them — and, the visible supply of Advertising Men who can write real "Salesmanship-on-paper " is mighty limited.

We serve several hundred clients, about three-fourths of whom are General Advertisers and one-fourth Mail-Order Advertisers.

And our experience with Mail-Order and other result-traced General Advertising, has shown that Space in Mediums is worth just what reasoning and conviction is put into it.

And because ours is the largest advertising business in America, we can afford to retain the ablest Copy-Staff in America, in addition to securing the best rates from Newspapers, Magazines, and Bill-Posters. Why don't you talk this over with us verbally?

Fortunes Wasted in Following "WILL-o'-THE-WISPS" - Article IX

MR. ADVERTISER! —

You've heard about "Keeping-the-Name-before-the People," and "Keeping-at-it?"

Well, that is "General Publicity" a Glory-Game, under a convenient alias.

"Keeping-the-Name-before-the-People," and "Keeping-at-it,"may incidentally "influence the sale" of goods, provided no competing line is being actually Advertised through "Salesmanship-on-paper."

But the main object of such "General Publicity " is less mercenary, more altruistic, than mere merchandising.

"Attract Attention;"— "Interest the Public" with pretty pictures and cute catch-words; — "Encourage the Publisher" by paying him for plenty of unoccupied white space; — and lastly, pay some Agency a commission to spend the money with the least effort and the most fireworks. That is "General Publicity,"— and it is well enough in its way, like the Carnegie Libraries.

But, what we object to, Mr. Advertiser, is that some folks, who ought to know better, call this altruism of "General Publicity" by the name of "Advertising."

Now, Advertising is simply plebeian "Salesmanship-on-paper" — a mere money-making means of selling goods by the quickest and cheapest method.

There is no Glory in this "Salesmanship-on-paper," — no applause for it, — no admiration, — just Profit. Because, it is simply common sense brought to bear directly upon the selling of Goods. That is its province — just selling goods over the counter or by mail.

If you want to find out how few goods "General Publicity" Copy ("Keeping-the-Name-before-the-People") will actually sell, test some of what you are now using, in a Mail-Order way, — to sell goods, mark you, — not merely to give away presents.

That is the test that shatters advertising Idols and dispels "Publicity" illusions.

You may have the smoothest "Catch-phrase" that ever happened, — you may be thoroughly tickled with Witty Wording, Pretty Platitudes, and Artistic Illustrations.

You may feel Cock-Sure that you have a kind of Advertising which couldn't fail (so long as the Salesmen do its work in addition to their own) . But, suppose you should try to actually sell goods, by mail with it.

If your World-beating Advertisement, that everybody sees" and admires, costs you $2.00 per Inquiry — and if another kind of advertisement you "don't like at all" brings equally good Inquiries, in the same space and same mediums, at 40 cents each, then we've learned something we can never afford to forget.

That is the kind of experience which makes us "sit up," and think hard, before we recover from the jolt it gives us.

And, when we "come to" we then see a great white light.

Under this new light, some of the things we thought we knew before fade out into vapory "Will-o'-the-Wisps," and we long for things tangibly proven.

When we observe now a hoary old Mail-order Advertisement, that seems at first sight stupidly simple and countrified, we look twice into it, to see if it isn't carefully loaded with hidden Selling Effect and subtle Conviction, under its guise of rural simplicity.

If we note it running for months, and perhaps years, without change, we no longer jump to the conclusion that the Man who pays for it is merely a Chump, serving his costly apprenticeship to our own Guild of advanced Advertisers.

No, — we look closely at it now for the hall-marks of Salesmanship, and where we find it running for months, without change of copy, we conclude there is some potent reason for it.

Because, we then feel that, had we as sure a means of keeping "tab"on results as this Mail-Order Advertiser, we too might be using some stale copy in " General Advertising," instead of changing it often without evidence from bad to probably worse.

If we had tried over fifty different changes of copy that had pleased us better than the Stale One, and had found (as others have done) that Inquiries from them cost $1.20 to $2.90 each, we would be mighty glad to go back to the good old "Chestnut" which produced Inquiries regularly at 40 cents average.

(See article herein entitled, "Why Some Advertisers Grow Wealthy, while Others Fail.") We would look upon that Ancient Adlet in the light of a tried and trusted Friend.

If we were asked to sell out our business we would appraise that bit of much-used Ancient History at a price that would make many Ad-smiths gasp.

And, why shouldn't we appraise it high up in the thousands.

If we spend $100,000 per year for Space, and fill that Space with copy that costs $1.20 per inquiry, (by mail, or over the counter), we get only 83,334 chances of Sale out of our appropriation.

With the Antique Adlet, or its skillful equivalent, our $100,000 would have produced 250,000 Inquiries, at an average of 40 cents each. These 250,000 Inquiries would have cost us $300,000 to secure at $1.20 each. (Which kind of copy are you using to-day, Mr. Advertiser?)

Why isn't the proven **40-cent"Advertisement worth all it saves, viz., $200,000 per year, so long as it continues to produce Inquiries averaging 40 cents each, instead of at $1.20 each?

Well, — why isn't such an Advertisement worth more than the space, Mr.

General Publicity Advocate?

***

What is the "something" in a successful Mail-Order Advertisement that makes it pull Inquiries at low cost?

It is the same "something" that would make it sell goods over the Retailer's counter, through General Advertising at correspondingly low cost.

That mysterious "something" is just Printed Persuasion, and its other name is "Salesmanship-on-paper."

It is the sapient ** something" that makes one Advertiser rich in a few years, while lack of it ruins others who buy their Space equally 'cheap, pay 5 per cent less commission, and spend equally large appropriations.

That "something" is Lord & Thomas "Reason-why" and Conviction, saturated into the copy, so that the Reader must believe the statements of merit thus claimed for the article.

Mere brilliance in Advertising fails utterly to produce profitable results (sales) if it lacks conviction. The "seeing," "admiring," or "reading with interest," of an Advertisement by the Public, avails little in dollars and cents, to the man who pays for the space, if it fails to CONVINCE the Public.

And, that conviction can be imparted, without accident, at will, by the few Advertising Men who have closely studied the thought-processes through which Conviction is induced, provided they have had the guiding light of experience with the facilities for comparing Results obtained from a large variety of Mail-Order Copy.

These results have invariably shown that it is far better to repeat one single Advertisement fifty times, if it be full of Conviction, than to publish fifty different Advertisements that lack as much Conviction, no matter how attractive, clever, or artistic, they may be.

In other words, one sound, convincing Advertisement will sell far more goods than fifty brilliant, catchy, strikingly displayed "Ads" that have less conviction in them.

The only mission of true General Advertising is to Sell Goods by driving the People to the stores armed with such reasons and convictions that substitution will be impossible.

And, when advertising is not selling goods, (through Conviction,) it is not doing as much as it can be made to do.

Any Advertiser who accepts mere "General Publicity" or "Keeping-the-Name-before-the-People " for his money, when he might have had all that and a positive selling force combined with it, is therefore losing half the results he might have had from the same appropriation.

We want to tell you more about this, verbally.

How Shall We Know Good Copy? - Article X

BY the Goods it is actually known to Sell, — Mr. Advertiser!

Don't care how "Bright, "how "Catchy," nor how " Attractive" the copy is, or is not.

What we want to know is how much Goods will it Sell, per dollar of cost, through Retailers or by Mail?

Selling-power is the only quality we recognize as Good , in Advertising.

No mere "Keeping-the-Name-before-the-People" will satisfy our standards.

No mere "Trade Stimulus" nor "General Influence on Sales" will we recognize as real Advertising worth what it costs.

No evasion of the Grand Issue — Salesmanship — is permitted nor attempted in the Lord & Thomas Advertising Shop.

The Ad-smith whose copy won't actually and positively Sell Goods enough to pay for the Space it fills, with a handsome profit on it to the Man who pays the Bills, is working for some other Agency.

But "how can we know copy which will positively sell goods, before it is published at the Advertiser's expense?"— you ask.

Well, this is how we know it, Mr. Advertiser!

About one-fourth of the Advertising we place annually is Mail-Order Advertising, for scores of different clients.

Every single insertion of each Mail-order Advertisement for these clients has been keyed separately, in each publication. We thus know precisely how much each Inquiry for goods Costs, from each different piece of Copy, in each Medium.

This information we"Record accurately in our "Record of Results." Then, we compare the Cost of Selling each line of Mail-Order goods through the different kinds of copy used, and we find a wonderful consistency in the figures.

A kind of Copy which produces Inquiries at low Cost for one proposition, we find produces Inquiries for another entirely different proposition in the same ratio of low cost.

And the kind of Copy which Costs three times as much per Inquiry, in the same publication, for one proposition will, we find, cost practically in the same high ratio on all other propositions.

The compilation of this data, covering a period of years, on a large variety of Mail-Order accounts, has given us a reliable means of knowing just what kind of copy Sells the most goods for a given investment in space.

It also affords us a reliable index to the relative Earning Power of different publications, using the same kind of Copy, at the same period of the year.

But, Lord & Thomas's investigation through this "Record of Results" has gone farther than testing out Mail-Order Copy.

Because, when the qualities, in Copy, that produced consistently large Results in Mail-Order Advertising had been located and isolated, these same qualities were then applied to Copy for General Advertising of Goods to be sold through Retailers.

Our "Record of Results" thus shows that the something which made a given kind of Copy sell goods at lowest cost by mail also made it sell goods at lowest cost through Retailers.

These qualities were "Reason-Why" and "Conviction" saturated into the Copy, and presented in certain thought-forms that strikes the most responsive cord with average Readers of Advertisements.

The combination of these qualities, evolved through our "Record of Results," is a formula as exclusive with Lord & Thomas as the formula of the famous Liqueur Chartreuse with the Monks who control its secret.

This kind of Copy we call "Lord & Thomas' Salesmanship-on-paper."

The relative Selling-Power of each piece of this copy we can judge in advance, by comparing it with Results obtained previously through kindred kind of Copy, used for equivalent Propositions, as registered and compared in our "Record of Results."

Let us show you a sample card from this Index to Results.

They Who Blindly Follow the Blind - Article XI

CARLYLE compared Mankind to a Flock of Sheep.

Stretch a rope across a country path, he said, about a foot and a half from the ground.

Then drive a flock of Sheep over it!

When the Bell-wether (or leader) has jumped that elevated rope, lower it to the ground and note what happens.

Every sheep in the flock that follows will jump a foot and a half in the air over that same rope, though it now lies slack on the earth.

They follow the Bell-wether blindly, — unreasoningly, — without regard to changed conditions.

They don't jump for the same reason that the Bell-wether jumped, nor for any other reason, but just because they saw another Sheep jump a given height, at a given spot.

Carlyle's comparison fits the Advertising situation like a blister.

There be flocks of Sheep innumerable in the Advertising field, Neighbor!

When Sapolio used the "Spotless Town" jingles, merely to revive mental impressions created by previous logical advertising, the flock of Sheep ran amuck on jingles, regardless of their application to other purposes.

When "Uneeda Biscuit" appeared on the market to fill a colossal waiting demand for a five-cent package, it was backed by an appropriation the mere volume of which must create a sensation (whether it sold goods or not) .

It, in turn, was followed by a brood of idiotic trade-marks launched on the Advertising field after it and because of it. When "Ivory Soap" Publicity appeared on the scene, with its full pages of pretty pictures, and its Five per cent of Selling Effect, the Sheep concluded that too must be "the best ever" in Advertising, so they promptly got in line and leaped the imaginary rope.

Then we had an epidemic of empty catch-phrases, following hard upon "Good Morning! Have you used Pears' Soap?" This, regardless of the fact that Pears' much parodied phrase had a foundation of a hundred years in accumulated advertising to tide it over its period of mental aberration. Where are these false Gods of Advertising to-day?

"Spotless Town" is off the map, and Hand Sapolio is now being advertised on the good old reason-why basis that built House Sapolio.

The old-time brood of "Try-a-bita," "U-want-a," and such other Uneeda chickens, has gone home to roost long before the tolling of Curfew bell.

"Uneeda Biscuit" itself, with the millions of Trust money behind it, can afford to keep up the Publicity bluff better than it can afford to admit the mistake of starting it.

But there are, every now and then, unwilling admissions of a Change of Heart, in such of their advertisements as "The Food Value of a Soda Cracker."

And where is that meteor of General Publicity "the Cremo Cigar," which flashed across the horizon of Advertising, with its million-dollar outlay for Bill-Board display in Newspaper space?

It, too, has gone into eclipse.

The American Tobacco Co., which "paid the Piper" for Cremo "Publicity" is now using for its United Cigar Stores, the "Reason-Why" copy it should have used from the beginning for "Cremo" Cigars.

Study the Ivory Soap advertising of the present and watch it for the future.

You will find in it, month by month, less pointless picture, and more "reason-why," though its owners will hate to admit the change of attitude their experience has induced.

Pears' Soap no longer says "Good Morning,"nor quotes, in place of it, any other catch-phrase. Yet, their once famous line is enshrined forever in the minds of old Fogy Advertising Men, who swear by the Pears' catch-phrase, but who never buy Pears' Soap as a result of it.

Meantime these Stars in the firmament of General Publicity, partially listed above, have lighted the way to ruin for a few dozen flocks of Sheep who thought they were following reliable "Bell-wethers" when they were only following Fads.

And, every new Fad, started in a large way by any big Advertiser (who has money enough to bum a big Bluff, and pride enough to sustain that Bluff till he can quietly change his play), will be applauded, copied, and "advised" by the Advertising Agencies who do not themselves understand the Compass, and so must follow the lead of others.

***

But, "'is there," you ask," any reliable Compass by which an Advertiser's barque may be safely and surely steered to success?" There is, we answer, a Guide as reliable to the Advertiser as the Compass to the Mariner.

That Guide is not available for Individual Advertisers who place their own business, nor for any other Advertising Agency but Lord & Thomas.

Its guidance is not based upon mere Opinion, nor on Guess-work, nor on Star-gazing.

It is based upon a carefully kept"Record of Results derived from Actual Tests made with different kinds of copy, in different mediums, and compared year after year on scores of different Advertising Propositions.

No Individual Advertiser could, with even the most carefully kept"Records, have more than a fractional opportunity to judge, by this infallible means, the kind of Copy, and the Mediums, that consistently produce the most results for a given outlay.

Because, each Individual Advertiser has only the experience which one single account affords, even if he had made perfect"Record of Results from it.

The Law of Average demands a greater range of experience than one proposition affords in order to safely weigh all the influences that bear upon Success, or failure, in Advertising Copy and Mediums.

We plan, and place, advertising for hundreds of clients, and we spend for them Several Millions per year, in a wide range of mediums.

Of this sum about one fourth is spent in Mail-Order Advertising, for a number of small and medium-sized accounts.

Now "Mail-Order" is to "General Advertising" what Surgery is to Medicine — an exact science, not a speculation. Every piece of Mail-Order copy we issue is keyed separately, and differently in each medium.

By this means the exact earning power of each piece of Copy, may be told by the number of Inquiries it produces for a given cost, and the number of direct Sales that result from it.

Not only this, but the relative earning power of each publication is accurately revealed by the Cost of Inquiries and Sales, through each particular medium in which the same copy is run, without regard to mere circulation claims.

The results from any one Mail-Order account using a given kind of copy, might only indicate the effectiveness of that kind of copy for that particular article.

This would afford no conclusive evidence as to how that kind of copy might work with a different sort of Mail-Order proposition, or in General Advertising.

But, when a given kind of Copy produces almost a uniform kind of Result for different Mail-Order accounts, and does it consistently for a year, it means something definite and indisputable.

And, when that same kind of Copy is tried out in General Advertising, for goods sold through Retailers, with the same consistent sort of Result, (judged by"Records of Comparative Sales in different, but equivalent territory) , it, too, proves something definite and conclusive.

No Agency in the World, and no Individual Advertiser, has ever made such exhaustive Tests on Copy, and on Mediums, as Lord & Thomas have made in the past few years.

No other Agency has ever gone to a tithe of the expense we have to compile careful"Records of these continuous Tests, so as to reduce the Writing of Copy and Choosing of Mediums, to almost an exact science.

These Lord & Thomas'"Records prove that a difference of 30 per cent to 80 per cent in Results exists between Copy which even we (with a previous experience of over 20 years) once thought good ourselves, and very different Copy that we now know to be good, every time, in every case.

This latter is not the kind of Copy that Agencies prefer to supply, because it costs five times as much to produce as catchy "General Publicity"costs. Moreover, it is the quiet, common-sense kind of copy which commands little glory for its creators, and few laurels for the Agency that uses it, except the continuous patronage of clients.

There are not fifty Advertising men in America who could write this kind of copy, even with the guidance our priceless "Record on Results" supply.

There are not four Advertising men who could write it so as to produce the Lord & Thomas result every time with-out the guidance of these particular"Records.

Of the fifty men in America able enough to write our kind of "Salesmanship-on-paper" under our direction, based upon these reliable Lord & Thomas"Records, we have fourteen continually on our Copy-Staff.

To these fourteen Copy Writers, capable of interpreting our experience into Lord & Thomas's "Salesmanship-on-paper," we pay an annual salary of $72,000 per year.

That is over three times as much as any other Advertising Agency pays for Copy-Staff, and five times as much as the average paid by any one of the five largest competing Agencies.

Not one of these competitors possesses the priceless advantage of our "Record of' Results" which make the services of each Copy Writer worth three times what the same services would be worth without them — and which eliminates the lottery element from Advertising.

We are telling you this, Mr. Advertiser, in clear-cut, definite terms, because you wanted to know if there was "any reliable Compass by which an Advertiser's barque might be steered safely and surely to success."Our "Record of Results" is the Compass, and our Pilots are properly trained to use it.

Without such a Compass, all Advertising Copy and Selection of Mediums, must be mere Gambling — sailing by the Starlight of baseless Opinion, Guess-work, and experiment.

Why then Gamble in "General Publicity " — in keeping the Name before the People whether your Advertising pays you or not, when the clear Sunlight of our "Records of Results" is at your disposal for your sure guidance?

When you place your Advertising through us we supply you the vital Salesmanship-on-Paper (that costs us $72,000 a year) to fill that space with, and to bring back your money with a sure profit on it.

Sometimes we decline an account if, on going over it, we decide that it cannot be made a success through Advertising. But, we refuse very few for this reason, because we have found it possible to make large successes of many previous failures, by applying our "Record of Results" — experience — to them.

Competing Advertising Agencies will tell you that we are "too Cock-Sure about Advertising" which they claim is an uncertain game at all times.

We are so "Cock-Sure" on this subject of Advertising, because we have that positive knowledge of Result-production which alone makes it possible to be "Cock-Sure."

The non-committal uncertainty of most Advertising Agencies (as to Results) springs from the most natural of causes — viz.: a knowledge that they do not know how to insure Advertising success.

That is why there is such a difference between the terms of your last Advertising Contract and ours, which we want to show you.

Making Sure of Results from General Advertising

MR. GENERAL ADVERTISER!

The first tangible Return from your money, when invested in Space, whether that Space be filled with "General Advertising" or with "Mail-Order Advertising," is an Inquiry for your goods.

That Inquiry may be verbal to a Clerk over the Counter, or — it may be by Mail, in a written, stamped, and posted letter.

But, in either case, it is just an Inquiry for the goods, of one sort or another. It is the first practical evidence that the money spent is earning something tangible for you in return.

Now — it may take twice or three times as much Conviction in Copy to make a Consumer write an Inquiry for goods, and post it, as it would have taken to make that same Consumer inquire verbally for the goods advertised, when passing a store that should sell them.

But, when he does inquire verbally from a Retailer, there are twice or three times as many chances of substitution, of "don't-keep-it " or "here's-something-better," as there would have been if that same Consumer had written direct for it; by Mail.

Therefore, the Advertisement which sends Consumers to Retailers, should be as full of Conviction as the successful Mail-Order Advertisement in order to fortify that Consumer against substitution, "don't-keep-it," and "here's-something-better."

Because, if the Advertisement fails to thus fortify the Consumer with "reason-why" and Conviction, it may simply send him to a Retail Store, to be switched on to a competing line of goods with which the Retailer is heavily stocked, or which his Clerks favor the sale of in preference to ours.

In that case the Advertising we pay for would sell goods for our non-advertising Competitors.

Half the money spent to "Keep-the-Name-before-the-People" results to-day in this substitution of non-advertised articles for the articles advertised through General Publicity.

"General Publicity" Copy, when tested, is found in almost every case too Weak to sell goods profitably by Mail. And any copy which is not strong enough, nor convincing enough, to sell goods by mail, is not strong enough to make the Consumer resist substitution, and the "don't-keep-that-kind" influence of Retail conditions.

"General Advertising" Copy, to succeed profitably, must therefore cause not only a verbal Inquiry for the goods, but must also have enough strong conviction saturated into it to make the Consumer insist upon getting the goods he asks for, against probable substituting influence.

It must therefore give him better "reasons-why" he should buy our goods than he is likely to hear from the retail Salesman for the competing goods that Salesman may want to substitute.

And, it must give him these "reasons-why" in such a lucid thought-form as he can understand without effort, so impressively that he will believe our reasoning Claims. I It must also do this in spite of his natural distrust of all Advertised statements.

This means that we must put into General Advertising Copy the precise qualities that would be necessary to sell goods profitably by mail.

Half the people who inquire for Advertised goods out of Curiosity as a result of "General Publicity "("Keeping-the-Name-before-the-People," etc.) do not buy them when they see them.

Because the competing goods will look just as fine when shown and recommended by the Substituting Salesman, and the Curiosity Inquiry, having no firm foundation of "Reason-Why"under it, cannot combat the personal influence of the Salesman.

This is why not more than a fourth of those who, out of mere curiosity, buy the first package ever buy the second or third consecutive package of the same article, through "General Publicity." Because they do not buy on Conviction.

Meantime, it usually takes about all the profit in the first purchase of any "Generally Advertised" article to pay the cost of introducing it to the Consumer's notice through Advertising.

But, with Lord & Thomas' "Salesmanship-on-paper" (Copy) results are insured and far more cumulative.

Because, a Consumer need only be convinced once, through our "reason-why" Salesmanship-on-paper," that the article is what he should, for his own sake, buy and use.

When we thus convince him, we achieve more than fortifying him against substitution. Because, we also help his imagination to find and recognize, in the article advertised, the very qualities claimed and proved for it in the Copy.

These qualities he might never have discovered for himself, nor appreciated, if he had casually discovered them, in a mere "Curiosity" purchase.

Because his attention had only been "attracted," not compelled and enduringly impressed with a logical understanding of these qualities.

But, when we once convince him, in advance of purchase, through our "Salesmanship-on-paper" (Copy) that the qualities claimed for the article do exist in them, he starts using that article with a mental acceptance of these qualities.

And, because he begins using the article with an advance knowledge of, and belief in, its good points, his appreciation becomes permanent if the goods merit it.

He therefore makes a second, third, and turtlier consecutive purchase of that article as a result of having once read a single convincing "Reason-Why " advertisement about it.

This is where large and cumulative profits must come to the General Advertiser — on the second, third, and continued purchases by readers of the first advertisement that reached their Convictions.

These conviction qualities in copy are shown, by test, to be just as necessary in Advertising designed to sell goods profitably to-day, through Retailers to Consumers, as they are to sell goods direct by mail to Consumers.

This is why every Advertisement for goods to be sold through Retailers, against substitution, and "don't-keep-it" influences, should have as much positive selling force, "reason-why"and conviction in it, as would be necessary to sell the goods by mail direct to Consumers.

The difference in Results from Space in which this direct selling force of Lord & Thomas' "Salesmanship -on -paper" has been used, and in results from similar space filled with "General Publicity,"is often more than 80 per cent.

Conclusive tests on Copy have clearly proved this, and one of our articles entitled "Why Some Advertisers Grow Wealthy," cites a vivid example of it, from actual experience.

Any Advertiser who is willing to accept mere "General Publicity" for his money, when he might have had all that and, in addition, a positive selling force combined with it, for five per cent more cost, is losing 50 per cent to 80 per cent of the results he might have had from the same identical appropriation.

Three-fourths of the salaries paid by most Agencies go to strong Solicitors who sell you Space, — and promise you service free of charge.

But, do the Solicitors' services as Salesmen help to bring your money back through the Advertising you must pay for?

Not 25 per cent of Advertising Agency salaries are invested in Copy Staff capable of making the Space sold by the Solicitors pay a profit for the Advertiser.

Could we afford to direct your attention to these facts if we were not the only exception to the rule cited?

The selling tests we have made on various kinds of Copy, and on most mediums, have convinced us that Salesmanship in "Copy" is the Heart and Soul and Essence of Advertising.

We have proven by these tests that even a poor medium, at a relatively high price, with strong "Salesmanship-on-paper" in it, will outsell the best medium using "General Publicity."

Our"Records-of-Results leave no doubt of this, while they also show which mediums sell the most goods per dollar invested, with the same kind of copy.

It has cost us nearly $100,000 to collect, compile, compare, maintain, and practically apply the reliable data upon which our judgment of Copy and Mediums is now based in our "Record-of-Results."

No other Advertising Agency, nor individual Advertiser, has any such reliable guide to go by, as this collection of organized data, nor such sure knowledge of Copy, and Mediums, as that sure Index affords.

And that Index to Results is what decided us to spend $72,000 per year in salaries, for a Copy Staff which is able enough to write the Lord & Thomas "Salesmanship-on-paper." No other Agency in America spends one-third of this sum for capable Copy-writers.

And, not three other Agencies individually, spent a fifth of it.

Will you see our representative and learn more about our "Record of Results"?

Intensive Advertising

Intensive Advertising Defined - Chapter 1

The term "Intensive Advertising" is new.

So we will explain it here -- by analogy.

And we will take for our demonstration a very practical example of "Intensive"

Policy, viz. -- Intensive Gardening. As commercially practiced in the suburbs of Paris, France by 1200 or more "Maraichers." These have for years cultivated market gardens that, in productiveness, are among the wonders of the world.

Such gardens average only about two acres each. But of these two acres are taken annually more vegetables through intensive cultivation than could be taken from one hundred acres by the usual methods.

Many of these tiny gardens are located on vacant city lots. On just such suburban lots as we, in America, devote to the gentle art of bill-posting, or to the careless culture of the ripe tomato can.

***

The ground rents paid by the "Maraichers" average about $200 to $250 per year, per acre. That for the use of the bare, unfertilized and often miserably poor soil,--as a foundation.

But production, through intensive culture, is so enormous that it is highly profitable even at such rentals. For those Intensive gardens are in reality nature-factories.

So abnormally great is their productiveness that they can only be thought of as making vegetables by steam.

Fifty tons per acre is a common output yearly.

Think that into pounds, viz. -- 100,000 per acre.

Seven huge crops per season, instead of the customary one, or at most two, crops under conventional methods.

The average gross income is $1500 per acre from these "vegetable factories." Ranging up to $6,000 per acre yearly, in some cases.

That -- my dear Sir, is -- "Intensive Gardening."

***

Now here's the rub!

All that this intensive principle means to gardening it can and does mean – when properly applied -- to Advertising.

When the self-same policy of deliberate concentration, thoroughness, and elimination of waste, is applied to advertising as faithfully and intelligently as it is applied to gardening intensively.

Salesmanship Multiplied - Chapter 2

What is good advertising? Merely Salesmanship multiplied.

Multiplied mechanically, by the Printing Press.

With the salary of a single Salesman, it is now possible to reach 1,000 probable customers for every individual that Salesman could have reached personally.

And with the self-same Selling Talk.

But, -- for all this it does not supplant the Personal Salesman. It increases his value instead. By doing the lesser "missionary" work at a lower cost than he could afford to do it. Thereby conserving his time and energies for the more profitable work of climaxing Sales.

Just as machinery, in mills, increased the earning power of Operatives. By increasing their productiveness.

Advertising is nothing more than Salesmanship.

But good Advertising is Salesmanship intensified. So as to compensate for the necessary absence of the personal magnetism of the Personal Salesman.

Wasteful methods are out of place today. And to fill costly advertising Space with anything less than Intensified Salesmanship is to waste Space. By wasting larger possibilities from that Space.

For this reason we must now dismiss the fatal fatuity of merely "Keeping the Name before the People." Which is less than a fifth part of Advertising possibility obtainable from the selfsame Space, and at the self-same cost.

Observe the mortuary"Records in such wasteful use of potential Advertising Space,

"Sunny Jim" is dead.

"Spotless Town" is off the map.

"The Smile that Won't Come Off" came off and never came on again after the money was spent.

"The Great firm of John Jones & Co." is out of business through too much "Keeping the Name of Jones before the People" and too little Salesmanship in the advertising.

All of which demonstrates for the thousandth time that Advertising Space, even in the best mediums, is not Advertising but only a receptacle for the conveyance of Salesmanship. Space can only multiply the precise percentage of Salesmanship we type into it.

***

Properly used, Advertising space is about the cheapest commodity in general use today.

Improperly used it is the dearest.

For Space is merely a multiplier.

Put 2% of Salesmanship into it, with 98% of "guff" and that 2% will be multiplied by as many thousands of readers as the advertisement attracts.

Put 98% of Salesmanship into it and the Space will produce just 4,800% more of Results for the self-same investment.

It is Sales-Influence alone that we buy Space for. And "Sales-Influence" is only another name for Salesmanship. Good advertising is, therefore, good Salesmanship. But, intensified, so as to compensate for lack of the Personal Salesman's personal magnetism.

Good Advertising is News - Chapter 3

Consider the Newspaper!

Which items in it do you read first? Not always those with the screaming flare-heads. Because Display alone is no longer interesting. It is News-Interest that attracts Readers now.

Without that commanding News-Interest display would merely cause us to "see" the article. But "seeing" and reading are two different matters.

We "see" many things from the street car windows that we are not even conscious of having seen.

We "see" them without realizing them, absorbing them, or being influenced by them in the slightest degree. They leave no"Record on the mind.

And so it is with mere Display in Advertising.

Without News-Interest display is largely wasted. And with sufficient News-Interest in the title, extravagant Display is entirely unnecessary, -- a mere waste of Space.

Remember this always, -- Display alone, be it ever so extravagant, cannot compensate for lack of News-Interest in the heading. It cannot compel conviction, or germinate a Buying Impulse in the mind. The advertisement which would profitably sell goods today must be read with as much interest as news.

It must stir Thought -- prompt buying Impulse -- and inspire Action upon that Impulse.

So -- "getting seen" helps little if the Advertisement accomplishes nothing more tangible than that.

***

Active News-Interest is therefore a first essential in the title of the Ad.

And with that essential secured, a moderate size of type for title, and a reasonably solid setting of "news-type" for body is entirely effective without heavy waste for white space and fancy borders.

Familiar news-type typography is more inviting to the eye than billboard Display at close Newspaper range. Certain of the simple old-style types, of moderate size, are so legible and familiar that they read much more freely than larger type of later styles. In fact, they almost read themselves, at first glance, with practically no eye-effort.

When a live News-Interest, expressed in primer thought, is set in such familiar size and style of type the message becomes so absorbent it almost soaks in irresistibly.

This with even quick and casual reading.

Straight Shop Talk can be dressed so as to overflow with News-Interest for the class aimed at.

If this were not true, Salesmen could not get a hearing for the self-same kind of Shop Talk with previously uninterested prospective customers.

No item of news is likely to be more interesting to a Manufacturer than an advertisement which reveals to him an easy means of reducing the cost of his product -- improving it without added cost -- or increasing his profits. And no article offered for sale, through Advertising, is likely to be devoid of some such News-Interest as that.

News-Interest for the class of Readers that constitutes the natural market for the article advertised. The Interest need not extend beyond that class, all other Readers being negligible, in Advertising.

Good Advertising is Plain Salesmanship Intensified.

A keg of Nails may be "just a keg of Nails" to a mere "Order-Taker." But -- to a real Salesman that keg of Nails bristles with characteristics. To him, these Nails are made of a certain kind of metal, by a certain kind of process, and will do certain things better than any other Nails on the market at the same price.

Moreover, he can tell you why they will do these things better, and other facts about them that our "Order Taker" ne'er dreamt of. Although he could, should and would have studied up and known all about these Selling Points if he had the instinct of the Salesman, with the industry to utilize it.

***

The Advertiser, or Salesman-on-Paper, who would win success today, through the printed page, must realize, and act upon the following facts, viz: -- He must vitalize his Advertising with active News-Interest, profitable Information and clinching Reason Why.

Before he can hope for notable, or even noticeable, results from the money he spends for Space. He must realize that competition is as keen today in Printed Salesmanship as it is in Personal Salesmanship. And that mere "Keeping-the-name-before-the-People" (with the sort of Publicity it stands for) is as weak and profitless today in competitive Advertising as mere "Order-Taking" would be in competition with strong, able and aggressive personal Salesmanship. "Good Advertising is News" first of all. But it is Salesmanship all the time.

How Short Should an Ad Be? - Chapter 4

That depends upon what it has to say!

If it has nothing to say worth reading, it should be mighty short indeed.

If it has no News-Interest, or no Information of value to the Reader, he will not go beyond the first few words. He will read just far enough to find out that the Ad. has nothing to say.

And the recognition of this accounts for the general attitude of too many Advertisers toward Advertising. They look upon it as necessarily and inevitably uninteresting.

Starting in with that assumption they assert that –

"Copy should be extremely brief."

"Consisting of a few words only."

"And these displayed in big black-faced type."

"With Splurge pictures and lots of white space."

Such is the popular impression of good Advertising.

"Blank's Whiskey, -- that's all!"

"Good Morning, -- have you used Blank's Soap?"

They are brief, -- and say nothing.

They might, with advantage, have been briefer yet. They might have said "Blank's Whiskey" or "Blank's Soap." And thus emphasized the brands further by the omission of the remaining words that say nothing worth saying.

"Cable Code Copy" is the pet name for this kind of General Publicity. Its use is a frank admission on the part of the Advertiser that People will not read more about their subject in the way they present it.

It is an acceptance of the thoughtless theory that Advertising is an imposition upon Readers. -- That People do not willingly read Advertising, and so must be clubbed into seeing it, whether they want to or not.

Its aim is to "Strike the Eye" instead of interest the Mind, educate and inform. So, it has been fittingly called "Eye-Deep" Advertising. The term supplies a correct key to its very superficial effect, -- its lack of Selling Influence.

***

How long should a good Advertisement be?

How long should a good Salesman talk to his Customer in selling goods? Just long enough to make his point. Just long enough to clinch the Sale, if that be humanly possible.

Provided he can make his Selling Talk interesting enough to hold his Customer's attention until the last word needed to climax what he set out to do. And no longer.

It is not necessary that the Selling Talk be interesting to the Bystander. Or any other than the Prospective Purchaser. It need not be of interest to "the Advertising world" at all. It need not be reckoned "catchy," "clever," "witty," or epigrammatic.

But -- it must sell or help sell goods.

It must leave on the Reader's mind a clear-cut impression of the best feature of the goods with a strong Buying Impulse toward them. Instead of leaving any diverting impression regarding the "cleverness" or other quality in the Ad itself or the Writer thereof.

Because, it is not the Ad that is to be sold but the Goods advertised in the advertisement.

This is where the "clever" catchy advertising of the "Eye-Deep" variety makes its most costly error. Costly to the Man who Pays the Bills.

It advertises the Advertising. Instead of advertising the Goods.

It leaves the Reader's Mind upon the "Catch Phrase," "striking picture," or other pyrotechnic Eye-Catcher. Instead of leaving it upon the desirable features of the Goods themselves, as the last and strongest and best-remembered impression.

Good Advertising should be conscientiously planned with the latter as sole objective.

In order to sell or help to sell the most goods for the least money.

***

To Sell Goods Requires Salesmanship.

And Salesmanship cannot be expressed without words.

So the rational course, in Advertising, is to use words enough, and space enough, to properly express proper Salesmanship for the article advertised. -- To produce an interesting reading, a firm conviction, and an active Buying Impulse after each Advertisement.

Not a word more than is necessary to do this.

And, not a word less.

The Boy who tried to knock the apple off the branch ten feet beyond his utmost reach with a stick only 9 ft. 11 inches was in a similar position to the Advertiser who starves his "Printed Salesmanship" for want of the necessary word or necessary space to make his Advertising effective.

If Advertising be given sufficient News-Interest, Information, and Selling force to pay the reader it can be made as long as the average Magazine Article, or Newspaper Editorial (if necessary) and with profit.

Between the strong Advertisement and the strong Editorial there is, after all, very little difference.

Both have a purpose to achieve with Readers.

Neither will be read unless it possesses sufficient news-interest, information or conviction to earn a reading.

And either can earn that if the subject and treatment be judiciously handled.

Brisbane's editorials are read by millions.

Talmage's Sermons were read by millions, in Newspapers alongside of and in open competition with "Live News Topics."

Lawson's chapters on "Frenzied Finance" in Everybody's Magazine were not short nor were his later Copper advertisements.

All of these were read from beginning to end by millions of busy people. Read for the News-Interest and Information they contained. Read because People found them worth reading.

And the self-same matter would have commanded the self-same reading in the Advertising columns if business motive had placed them there.

-- With similar title-interest and similar setting, the length of the articles would have been an attraction as indicating the probable importance of the subject.

A good Advertisement should be just long enough to accomplish its Selling Purpose. And no longer -- or shorter.

To Plan and Write Strong Ads - Chapter 5

Start with the Right Point-of-View.

Consider what Advertising is for. Viz. -- to help Sell Goods -- nothing less.

Write the copy with that object in mind.

Even if Salesmen are employed to close the sales.

Don't let yourself down to mere "Keeping the Name before the People."

Don't be satisfied to produce mere "Publicity." Because, -- if you do you will never achieve real strong vitalized Salesmanship-on-Paper.

And this to encourage you.

One good, strong, convincing piece of Advertising copy will sell, or help to sell, more goods than 50 pieces of "Eye-deep Publicity."

So take fifty times the time, if necessary to produce it. And if twelve run-of-mine ads were enough to do the job before, six such pieces of real virile Salesmanship-on-Paper, rotated, will do the job much better.

Good Mail Order Ads run without change for years on end. Because, no new Ads since written could approach them in actual Sales production per dollar invested for space. The proof of this is available if you want it. And that proof shows that the life of a really good and complete piece of copy is practically limitless.

***

Make up your mind to concentrate all your effort and all the material you possess upon the single Ad. you are writing at the time.

Intensify it, with every selling point you know of.

Don't try to save out essentials for other Ads of the series. Put all of the very best your closest study can provide into the single Ad you are then writing.

And when all has been skillfully incorporated, start in to prune it of unnecessaries.

Cut out every needless word first. Then cut out every selling thought that can be spared without weakening the Salesmanship.

Then review the whole work as coldly as your worst critic might. But, from the standpoint of your prospective customers only. Not from the standpoint of the mere Advertising World.

Disregard that entirely -- forget it. Because, it does not matter what the Advertising World thinks about your copy if you can make it sell goods profitably.

Because the Advertising World knows infinitely less about the proposition you are then working upon than you do.

That's if you earnestly and capably live up to the following formula.

***

First study your Customers.

Sit down, close the door, and leisurely think out who are the Natural Buyers of the Article to be Advertised.

Make a penciled list of some typical cases. Interview these typical cases.

Ask why they have not already bought the Article you are about to Advertise, or bought more of it.

Ask what objections they would probably raise against the article if a Salesman called upon them and tried to sell it to them.

Then list the probable objections.

And then find the most conclusive answer to these objections.

Next, compile all the Selling Points of the Article in question. And remember that its exclusive selling points are to be the backbone of your Salesmanship.

To say that a certain machine will cut ice would avail little in advertising it against competing machines -- all of which will cut ice. It will be necessary to tell how much ice it would cut in a given time. At a given cost per ton. And why. Contrasted with the cost by other Machines that cut ice at higher cost -- And why at higher cost.

***

Well, when all the selling points in our subject have been marshaled and listed, -- When all the objections which would probably be raised by our customers have been assembled and answered we are then ready to construct the case.

So we come back to a mental conception of the typical buyer of this Article again.

In order to know how best to approach him.

How best to interest him in the Ad. How best to get him "with us" in reading the Ad.

instead of "against us." In other words how to get him into a receptive attitude instead of into a combative attitude.

Next we estimate at what point our Advertised Article is most likely to touch his interest. Which, of all our selling features, are most likely to appeal to him strongest.

Then we make that feature the pivot upon which to swing the whole argument an all the other features in the order of their relative importance -- to him.

Now we start in to write the Ad. And we write it as if this was the only Ad we ever meant to use. We write it so that it is a complete selling canvass for the Article condensed into the fewest words that will express it.

This is the order of thoughts and requirements in writing it.

***

First -- News Interest.

The title and the first lines must be invested with this to command a reading for the Ad.

That "News-Interest" must be kindred, and entirely natural, to the subject matter.

Avoid by all means the far-fetched headings that disappoint the reader. Because, the revulsion following the feeling of being tricked would antagonize him against the Article advertised instead of leaving him favorable to it.

The News-Interest must therefore be evolved from the Subject itself. (Not faked-up from the outside and tied to it with a slender thread) And that News-Interest must exist somewhere in the subject itself or the Article could not be sold by any Salesman. A live News-Interest for the man who should buy the article, even if for no one else.

It is there -- in the Subject. So sit down and dig it out.

Then play it up in the title. As the only proper "Eye-Catcher." Which will be sure to catch the eye of the very men you want to reach with the Advertised article. Even if it interested no one else.

If the title now possesses enough live News-Interest, the first few lines only need be devoted to introduction of the subject.

Because, we should then jump into the facts at once. Playing up the most interesting feature, first, the most convincing one last. Expressing the whole matter in primer-thought, and in language forms so simple that even a child of twelve would fully understand all it meant.

The object of this simplified language is not merely to avoid misunderstanding. But, to make the absorption of the meaning effortless for the reader. To make it so apparent that the information will almost "soak-in" without any mental labor on his part.

And beyond this, there is a valuable quality in simple thought-forms and familiar language which should never be overlooked. Viz. -- its more ready acceptance as truth, when in these forms.

For some undefined reason elaborate phrasing, intricate thought-forms, and high sounding words seem to impart suspicion to the Reader.

Where the simpler and more familiar forms seem to disarm it and carry the message home without arousing so many unspoken questions.

Perhaps because simple language simply spoken is characteristic of Sincerity.

***

And Now For the Climax.

This is where the majority of otherwise good advertisements fail. They do not clinch.

Their last lines lack the vital active quality. That intensive quality which makes the Reader want to buy the article, and want to do something toward buying it at once.

There is only one place in the Ad. for the planting of this spur action -- And that is in the last sentence. Which sentence should be carefully thought out, and framed up to climax all that has gone before into an active Impulse toward buying.

Make the Reader do something definite toward purchase at that stage and you have committed him unconsciously to a partial acceptance of your statement from which he will not be likely to later hedge.

Moreover, having moved him to action through the printed Salesmanship, his mind"Records the impressions deeper because of that action. And he is henceforth more receptive to subsequent Salesmanship, printed or verbal, on the same subject.

He has imbibed the germ through your printed Salesmanship and it will henceforth "work while you sleep."

If it now be nursed along with occasional follow-up of consistent nature, he is in a fair way to become not only a Purchaser, but a well-informed advocate of the Advertised article.

If your Advertised Article be of a kind which you cannot reasonably hope to sell him through Printed Salesmanship, make it possible for him in the Adv. to do something toward purchasing.

And then make him do it. In the last clinching sentence.

***

The advertising man who tries to do no more in his advertising than to "keep the name before the trade" -- Who wastes space by wasting the larger possibilities from that space -- Reminds me of the "man who held four aces." And played them without looking at them. Winning what he should have won with his customary "pair of Jacks."

Which conclusion makes the punishment fit the crime. And is entirely satisfactory to the Writer of these articles. Who, with a much abler Writer, in a larger field, believes in -- "Letting every man go to hell after his own fashion."

Resources

Get the rest of the Masters of Marketing Series:

- Breakthrough Copywriter – A Field Guide to Eugene M. Schwartz Advertising Genius by Dr. Robert C. Worstell

- How to Write a Good Ad by Victor O. Schwab

- My Life in Advertising by Claude C. Hopkins

- Obvious Adams: The Story of a Successful Marketer by Robert R. Updegraff

- The Robert Collier Copywriting Course by Robert Collier

- Scientific Advertising by Claude C. Hopkins

- Tested Sentences That Sell by Elmer Wheeler

- The Untold Story of Advertising based on lectures by Albert D. Lasker

- The What, How, and Why of Advertising by – John E. Kennedy

- How to Sell Without "Selling" by Orison Swett Marden and Edward Berman

- How to Write Ad Copy that Works by Justus George Fredericks

Available from most online book outlets and in print.

Bonus

Get No-Charge Access to Our Business Guide Library

Instant Access - Join Here

Click or type into your browser:

http://livesensical.com/go/byob/

www.ingramcontent.com/pod-product-compliance
Lightning Source LLC
Chambersburg PA
CBHW021909170526
45157CB00005B/2024